COMING

by Paul Williams

Entwhistle Books

3rd printing and new LPI edition, July 1999

ISBN 0-934558-25-6

available from:

Entwhistle Books
Box 232517
Encinitas CA 92023

and from: www.paulwilliams.com

or: 760-753-1815

for you and me

Coming is the same as being.
It's what we're here for—
   there's nothing else to do.
Come with me. I'll tell you a secret.

The secret is: don't hold back.
I know— it doesn't work— you tried it.
But did you, really?
When it's time not to hold back,
   you shouldn't hold back **at all**.

There's so much to learn in this world!
I am starting to learn how to come.
I'm learning that it doesn't matter.
There is no end to this love we're making.
I may as well give you everything now...

How to come.

How to come:
   gracefully
   slowly
   passionately
   often.

How to come.
How to become.
How to keep going.
How to stop.

How to be.

There are two of us.

We are woman and man.
We are person and person.

We make love to each other
   only because we don't know how to stop.

Sometimes, we don't make love,
   only because we don't know how to begin.
It's better not to know how to stop.

God bless the things we don't know...

We don't know who we are.
We touch each other to find out.

We come to each other like students
   of a higher knowledge.

I would like to tell you everything I know
   about coming.
I would like to tell you
   everything I know.
I don't know why I feel this desire toward you.
It is not indiscriminate. It is for you alone.

It's late.

There is no one to talk to now.

When I'm alone, I am far away
   from our innocent romps together.

I get into the rhythm of being alone.

I like it.

I don't know what it's like to be you alone.
I don't want to know.
There are limits to intimacy.
I can only be you with me.

I love being you with me.

When it's late and I'm alone, I think about you
   and me
Becoming each other
And I feel love for myself

This is the secret

Now I know why we need each other

It is the story of our lives

We come apart

And then we come together.

There's nothing else to do.

Apart and together.

I do need you.

This is a song of love.

Testing the water. I'm searching for someone to talk to. My situation limits me, no question about it— just as living in the woods limited me when I was there, just as editing a magazine limited me when I was doing that. Whatever work we choose to devote ourselves to, whatever love we manage to express, it limits us but it also creates us, defines us, makes us real. If we throw away our limits, our constraints, we also throw away our only doors to the other side.

I keep telling myself, over and over again: **stop searching**.

Relax, friend.

Take a look at what you've found.

I keep rediscovering things. That's what I want to talk about. I keep rediscovering little parts of myself I'd forgotten about completely. I keep realizing I'm the same person I've always been—I remember the child, the teenager—and I want to reach out and take hold of these realizations, hang on to them, not forget this time. I want to be whole...whatever that is.

And I enjoy these rediscoveries. There is a fearful and wonderful pleasure in the shock of recognition.

I am a man upon the land. I heard these words in a song when I was in high school, and later forgot about them; but now I remember how much they meant to me. The song was saying one thing, but I heard something else: a man on the land, like a boat on the ocean, I'm set loose upon this planet, I am free.

My sails are open, and I follow my heart.

Yes, very romantic. But don't put me
down. And don't let me put myself down. I see
a spark of beauty and I want to suppress it.
And yet I say I want to be attractive to people.
How foolish of me.

Nurture the spirit. Or at least let it
be. There is this search for balance. I want
all the parts of me to coexist, to be visible,
to be alive.

It's a very ambitious undertaking.

"All the parts of me"—well, I mean a lot of different things by that. There are an infinite (or so it seems) number of parts which I recognize at different moments. They exist all at once, but I'm not sure I've ever been able to stand back far enough to see them that way.

We don't know ourselves very well. That's what makes these rediscoveries so exciting.

We **think** we know ourselves, and then **bam!** we run into stuff of major importance in our lives that we had forgotten about completely.

This is a book about coming.

It's also about the shock of recognition.

It's a book about getting to know myself.

The secret is: don't hold back.

I get to know myself by making love to you.

What kind of a world is this?
I was walking down the street—
   I saw my reflection in a store window—
And then I saw you there beside me.
How can it be that I see you so seldom
And yet we're always together?

(Do you still love me?)

Oh, I want to hold you now.

I am starting to learn how to come.

I'm learning how to relax when I'm excited.

And how to stay excited while I relax.

I'm learning to receive and give at the same time,
   without knowing which is which—

Are you giving to me or receiving from me?

Everything is both at once.

Everything is happening now...

Floating on my back
In the ocean
Looking back at the sun
I am coming

Now
It doesn't matter
Now
I want you so much
Now
I don't know who I am
Now
I am coming

We are going

Oh, I love to feel you!

We are gone...

And here we are together   on the other side

(soft landing
on another planet)

the world of after-sex.

Come with me. I will tell you what I've been doing all my life. I've been looking for you. I don't know why. Some things are beyond conscious reason. I don't care who you are. I just want to hold you. I don't know why this feels so good. Hold me a little tighter please. I've been so lonely without you. And yet so whole sometimes too. I really don't understand. It's just something I saw in your face. Can you feel it too? Isn't it strange... Who planned it this way...?

And who are you, to have such power over me?

And who am I, to be alone with you in this room?

Doesn't it feel like we're the only people in the world?

Everyone else must be wishing they were here too.

More to come.

There's always more
Of you and me
To come
(together)
If we don't hold back
There's always more
That is the best news of all.

You make me inexhaustible.

Everything I am
    is here
    at your command.

Your smile   moves me.

The energy I feel from your smile
Could turn the world
If we knew how to harness it

(and we do)

You and me
Is the source of all the energy there is.

I think of you sometimes.

When I speak of energy, I don't mean oil in the ground. I'm talking about human energy. Life energy. Whatever gets us out of bed in the morning. That's what makes the world turn.

Your smile, when I think of you, gives me energy I didn't have before. It's a miracle. Where did that energy come from?

Let's think of me as a bundle of potential energy. You're just a bundle, too. When we **get the feeling** of love towards each other, energy is released. A million years are gone in a moment.

We burn.

We reach out to each other, and set the world in motion.

This is what I believe: the problems facing us can only be solved by making better use of human energy. Any other solutions are trivial and worse than useless because they don't go to the heart of the matter.

The only way to act on this information—to turn theory into practice—is for each of us to dedicate ourselves to making better use of our own energies in our daily lives. It is not necessary that we work toward a common cause. That will come of itself if enough of us just focus in on our own real self-improvement.

Don't hold back.

When it's time to give, give everything.
When it's time to act, don't set aside some
part of your energy to save for a rainy day—
and then fail, and then say, ''I knew I couldn't
do it''—your actions are important, they need
to be done right. You can't afford to do any-
thing else but give all of yourself to right
action at this moment.

If this action fails, your future actions—
the ones you've been saving for—will be built
on a crumbling foundation.

Don't underestimate the importance of this moment.

It's the only moment there is.

Coming is the same as being.

Good sex is a state of mind.

Sometimes we try too hard. What are we trying to prove?

All we need do is be kind to each other.

If we can feel each other, it's easy to be kind.

If we **can't** feel each other, let's go back to the beginning and start all over again.

shape of my life

determined by strange movements

in my heart and loins

I want something

I don't know what it is

I want you

I don't know who you are

I just know what I want when I see it

and I don't know why...

I can't stop and think

I hesitate, but in the end it doesn't matter

I just have to come over and say

hello

I knew it would happen

we've been meeting this way for

thousands of lifetimes...

Why is it you
Your face seen once from a distance
That causes me to break my own chains
When no one else could do it?

I **wanted** to do it before
But this time I **had to**
And here we are in each other's lives...

Why is it you
When we're under the covers at night—
Holding your marvelous body
Why am I me?

I love being you and me.

I love to touch you, fingers and tongue
Body and body
Touching you all over, I get in touch with my self.

I feel whole.

I feel strong and loving, and I love the feeling.
Thank you.
You give me to me.

And then, when **you** touch **me**,
That is a miracle.
Excitement shoots through me,
how could I ever have imagined
another being would care about me?

You give me grace.

Your mysterious appreciation of me,
my body, your loving touch,
I can't believe it but I do accept it,
I want it, I love it—
You lift me up
and I float away.

We are magic.

In bed, or rolling on the floor

In the still of the night, or midday sun

We feel the spark, and go for each other

What a lovely brawl

It's magic, oh arms and legs

Everywhere, and sudden contact

Penetration and exaltation

Excitement beyond description

Gentle and loving and out of control

We are magic together, we are every body

We are coming

We are being

We are being, and we live in this universe.
We like it here.

You are being, because you are we.
Come with me, and you'll feel it too.

We are being, we are all-embracing.
Our parts are scattered far and wide.
You are we.
When you see yourself in your lovers' eyes
Embrace yourself
And be released.

Come.

Come home.
You are forgiven.

You are wanted.
Come.
We need you.
Come.
I need you.
I want you.
Come with me.
Oh, come.

Yes. Oh, yes.
Oh now
Oh...

Thank you for being you.

You're welcome.

To come is to approach.
Come. Listen.
What is it we approach?
When we touch each other, we approach the altar.

We come closer.

We reach toward that which is highest in us.

We reach toward
                spirit.

Fucking is a wholly spiritual activity.

spiritual

emotional

intellectual

physical

these are the four elements

once they were called, "the humours"

Fucking is wholly spiritual. It is also physical.
Never get out of touch with the physical.

Love is emotional. It is also intellectual
   ("it's all in your mind").

Making love is physical, and spiritual.

Mind, heart, body, and soul.

These are the four elements.

If two people can make contact
   in all four realms at once
   they will hold the universe in their hands.

When you hold the universe in your hands,
  you are God.

And then you let it go.

That's what God would do.

We come together.

And we come apart.

It is a song of love.

I keep realizing I'm the same person I've always been.
At first I thought it wasn't me you loved.
And then I started seeing me through your eyes.

Who is that person?

And when I recognized the stranger
  I felt humble and proud
  both at once

We are ladders
In coming, we climb each other
Toward an absolute
Climax
Certainty
Higher each time
Until we fall
                    into the infinite.

We are falling through the sky
Toward the stars.

Absolute fulfillment
Is emptiness
Reborn.

When I see you, and my thoughts turn lusty
And my
            involuntary   nervous   system
Begins to respond to you, to the idea of
   loving you
When that process starts (and it's hard to
   stop it)
I want to hold you
I just want to hold you, and I really don't care
About the price of flour
Or the price of love.
I want to spend all my energy
   in you.

And when you've taken all I have
And I am completely naked
And filled with emptiness
And we are alone together
The world gets very quiet
And if we stay awake
And don't say anything
I think we can hear
Its heartbeat

The heartbeat of the world
Sounds like two lovers
Who have fulfilled each other
And are ready to start again

You make me inexhaustible
World without end
Just let me close my eyes for a minute
And I'll sleep for a thousand years

or touch me lovingly
and again I'll be ready for anything

Coming = being
= you and me
together
again
for the first time

   forever.

Holy of holies
All is wholly
empty
            anyway
What am I doing here?

How did you get me into this?

What? You say **you** were following **me**?

Oh dear.

I think we're going around in circles.

(but it only makes you dizzy if you think about it)

(don't think about it)

(let it go)

Sometimes when I get trapped in thinking
If you hold me in your arms
It seems to help

I am starting to learn how to come.
Body comes.
Heart comes.
Mind comes.
Spirit comes.
Earth, water, air and fire
Come together to form the universe.

We touch each other
and form the universe.

We conceive
the inconceivable.

We give birth
to the world without end.

The more we're together
The better we are at making love to each other

But still, what excites me the most
Is the stranger in you.

The unknown is the root of fear.
It is also the home of desire.

I believe we will never fully know each other.

And so we can love forever.

Desire is a part of coming.

Love can exist on a purer plane.

But love-making needs desire.

I want you.

These are the holy words of sex.

It is lust for the world that creates the world

Every time.

It is not in my mind
All my sense-receptors are telling me
You're a desirable creature
You go to my head
I come to my senses.

We are sensual creatures.

We use the physical world
   as a door
   to all communication.

Desire is kindled in the heart and loins
   by information brought in
   from the senses.

We see each other
(hear touch taste smell)
And then we want each other

Little chemical reactions
   take place
   and change our lives.

We come together
Because we want each other
So much we can't stop
Sensual input spurs us on
Desire feedback overload breakthrough.

Coming.

And when we've exhausted desire
We fall through the sky together.

It's important to be alone.

I keep finding people and places I've known before
But hadn't seen or felt directly for a long time

And every time it's like the return of a long-lost friend—
   an intimate friend— a part of me.

I feel as though I'm a traveller in this world
Making the rounds like a squirrel in winter
Discovering treasures I'd forgotten I stashed
Way back last summer sometime.

And slowly, all the years of my life
Are coming back to me.

It all comes back.

I never could have dreamed my own future.

What brought us here tonight?

Accident and desire, courage and curiosity.

Affection.

love.

We are here because there's nowhere else to go.

It's important to be alone.

Sometimes it feels good
    to be alone together.

Feeling good
is also important
and sometimes
irresistible.

We fall towards each other.
We can't stop.

A body in motion stays in motion.

I am coming.

We are here tonight
because of gravity

Heavenly bodies attract each other
and fall together

Your tongue
touches my lips
and I must open to you

Arms around each other
We're holding on
    for dear life.

We're holding on
because what flows between us
feels so good
and won't let go

we fall towards the warmth in each other

nerve endings
brush nerve endings
pleasure is everywhere

I must open to you.
We're holding on
    to the sky.

It's so good to be with you again.

Retracing my steps. My state of mind is hard to describe. I feel very relaxed, and centered. Years have gone by, but it makes no difference. Seeing you again, I understand now that we were never apart. I was with you and you were with me and there was no time between. Always together. And isn't it nice that our paths have crossed again?

Every moment we get to spend together is a blessing. And with all my heart I am glad for this blessing, and respectful of the forces that have allowed it to happen.

We were meant to be together.

But we were also meant to be apart.

We are in motion
attracted to each other
but pushed apart
by opposing forces
inside ourselves
pulled apart and together
by the times and the changes
in our inner and outer lives—

Such an intricate dance!

And then suddenly the dance falls away
And here we are alone in this room.

I've been waiting all my life for this moment.

And I'd just like to
   prolong indefinitely
the magic that is happening
      now.

Let's stop some time together.

Let's not stop, this time...

It's too late to stop now.

We may as well keep being.

Being is the same as coming.
I'm beginning to understand.

Come with me.
I've missed you so much.
I need you now.

I want you
now.

I want
to be able
to touch you
everywhere

I want to just run wild with you.

I want your body
with you in it
responding to me
touching me
I want to make you feel so good
I want to be in that place again

It still amazes me
that you say you don't carry that place with you
and I know it's not here with me
and yet whenever we come together...

Whenever we're together
—sometimes when we're together—
there's this place that appears around us.
I can't tell you what it looks like,
but I know what it feels like.
It feels like I'm set free.
It feels like I can do whatever I want.
It feels like a magical land of childhood.
And you're here with me.
And all my energy
is for you.

And I know
our desire
to come
together
creates this universe.

Whatever it is
we feel towards each other
it's the greatest magic
there is.

And it's happening everywhere
  all the time
Any two people you see
  might be practicing this magic
It's hard to believe
  such forces can be loose in the universe
Storms of energy
  everywhere every minute
What a glorious mystery

How can all this coming be happening
  without tearing the universe apart?

I guess we tear it apart
  and rebuild it together
    every day.

When we're fucking, we're at the center of the universe.

Anyone who's been there knows it's true.

Come with me
and let's do it again.

I'm waking up
to find I've been here all along.

I've just arrived on a distant shore.

Why does it look so familiar to me?

I've never been here before.

I've never been anywhere but here.

This place
is utterly new and utterly familiar
both at once.

It makes me wonder
who I am.

How many times have I walked on this planet?
How many times have I lived this life?

Only once
but here it comes again.

Here it comes again.
Can't you feel the shock
of recognition?
Don't you see the firmament shaking—
trembling—

uncontrollable
passions
raging

through the Earth
as she gives birth
to her creatures—

every glorious moment
of our lives?

It is good

to be in love

with this life.

I am in love

with the Earth

and all her women

and men.

.

And children.

And all her other creatures—

animal, vegetable, mineral.

And most of all
I'm in love with the way
  everything
  fits together

—Like you and me,
  for example.

Whoever put us together

knows us

better than we know ourselves.

It's so good to be with you again.

It's so good to be

whoever

I am.

Thank you

for everything.

You're welcome.

BOOKS BY PAUL WILLIAMS:

Practical philosophy:

Das Energi
Remember Your Essence
Fear of Truth (*Energi*
    Inscriptions)
Waking Up Together
The Book of Houses (with
   astrologer Robert Cole)
Coming
Nation of Lawyers
Common Sense
How to Become Fabulously
    Wealthy at Home
    in 30 Minutes

Hippie memoirs:

Time Between
Apple Bay or Life on the Planet
Heart of Gold

Collections:

Pushing Upward
Right to Pass and Other
    True Stories

Music:

Performing Artist, The Music of
   Bob Dylan, Volumes I & II
Brian Wilson & the Beach Boys
   —How Deep Is the Ocean?
Neil Young—Love to Burn
Rock and Roll: The 100 Best
    Singles
Watching the River Flow:
   Observations on Bob Dylan's
   Art-in-Progress 1966-1995
The Map—Rediscovering Rock
    and Roll
Outlaw Blues
Back to the Miracle Factory

Other arts:

The 20th Century's Greatest
    Hits
Only Apparently Real: The
   World of Philip K. Dick

Edited by Paul Williams:

The International Bill of Human
    Rights
The Complete Stories of
    Theodore Sturgeon
(magazines: *Crawdaddy!*
The PKD Society Newsletter)

ALL in print. For a catalog or ordering information, contact:
Entwhistle Books, Box 232517 Encinitas CA 92023 USA
www.cdaddy.com (look for **Entwhistle Books** button)
phone or fax: 760-753-1815   email: EB@cdaddy.com

CPSIA information can be obtained
at www.ICGtesting.com
Printed in the USA
BVHW071941291221
625096BV00001B/147